# Is Ranger In Danger?

Diane Odegard Gockel

ISBN: 0989631761
ISBN 13: 9-780989-631761

**Dedication**

To our first grandchild, London Daniel Stafford. You light up the room and my life each time I see you. I am grateful to be able to spend so much time with you, watching you grow into the beautiful person you were created to be. I especially love enjoying the farm with you. Moo, baa, neigh!

Love,
Oma

And to Chase, our first rescue. We will miss you on the farm. You were always a true and loyal pup.

**About the Author:**

Diane Odegard Gockel is a former high school teacher who has devoted much of her life to the rescue, fostering, and adoption of homeless pets. She is a featured author for Microsoft's Skype in the Classroom, where she reads her Rescue Series books to children in classrooms around the United States and beyond. Diane and her husband have four grown children and two grandchildren and live on a small rescue farm in Sammamish, Washington.

**Other books in the Rescue Series by Diane Odegard Gockel**

The Rescue of Winks

Bella Saves the Farm

Al the Alpaca: Forever Friends

Fancy Has a Plan

Pat and the Gabby Goats

Cowboy and a Pig that's Not Too Big

## Is Ranger in Danger?

My name is Ranger, and I am one of the happiest, friendliest, and most playful pups you will ever meet, but my life did not start out that way at all. Almost from birth, my life and the lives of my brothers and sisters were very much in danger. We were in need of a rescue only three weeks after our birth!

My brothers and sisters and I were born outdoors, behind a shed at a warehouse. The owner there did not seem to care for animals. He would often shoo Mama away when she would beg for scraps from the workers as they ate their lunches. Much of her day was spent trying to find enough food to keep her strength to nurse us all.

When we were about three weeks old, all of us pups were cold and tired but too hungry to sleep as we lay in the wet grass waiting for Mama to feed us and keep us warm. After two days had gone by without Mama returning, one of the workers came by and picked each of us up and piled us in the bottom of a cardboard box. We were still cold and hungry when I heard the worker whisper to us with concern in her voice, "I will see if we can find someone to care for you pups before it is too late."

My siblings and I were too young to walk, and our eyes were just opening. We were scared. The worker carried our box to the side of the building and left. Soon, we felt just enough sunlight on us to warm up and doze off. We were all awakened by the sound of the worker talking to another woman.

"They are over here in a box," she said. "They have not eaten for two days. Perhaps you can save at least a few of them. Apparently, the mom dog passed away."

This was when we met the Farm Lady for the first time. I was on the bottom of the pile of pups but managed to wiggle my way to the top to see her face as she peered down with love and empathy.

"Oh, you poor babies!" she said. "Let's get you into a warm bed and get you out of this place."

The Farm Lady then gently picked each of us up, gave us our first human kisses, and placed us gently in a laundry basket on a warm, fuzzy blanket. I still remember how it felt…almost like snuggling with Mama. The Farm Lady drove us away, and we never went back.

As the Farm Lady's truck came to a halt, she gently lifted us out of the front seat and carried our cozy basket to the barn. She placed us and our blanket on the stall floor under the warmth of a heat lamp. She offered us a bowl of thick, creamy milk that smelled so good! We were so hungry, but we had never drunk out of a bowl, and we weren't sure how to do it. We stuck our faces in the milk, but we had not been taught to lick yet.

"I will try to feed you another way," the Farm Lady said with urgency before leaving the barn.

Soon, I heard the Farm Lady's voice and other voices. She returned with her daughter, her mother, and her aunt. They picked each of us up separately and spoon-fed us the warm, creamy milk. They also named us. They called me Ranger. We all ate as best we could and fell fast asleep with full bellies, snuggled in a pile on our fuzzy blanket under the heat of the lamp.

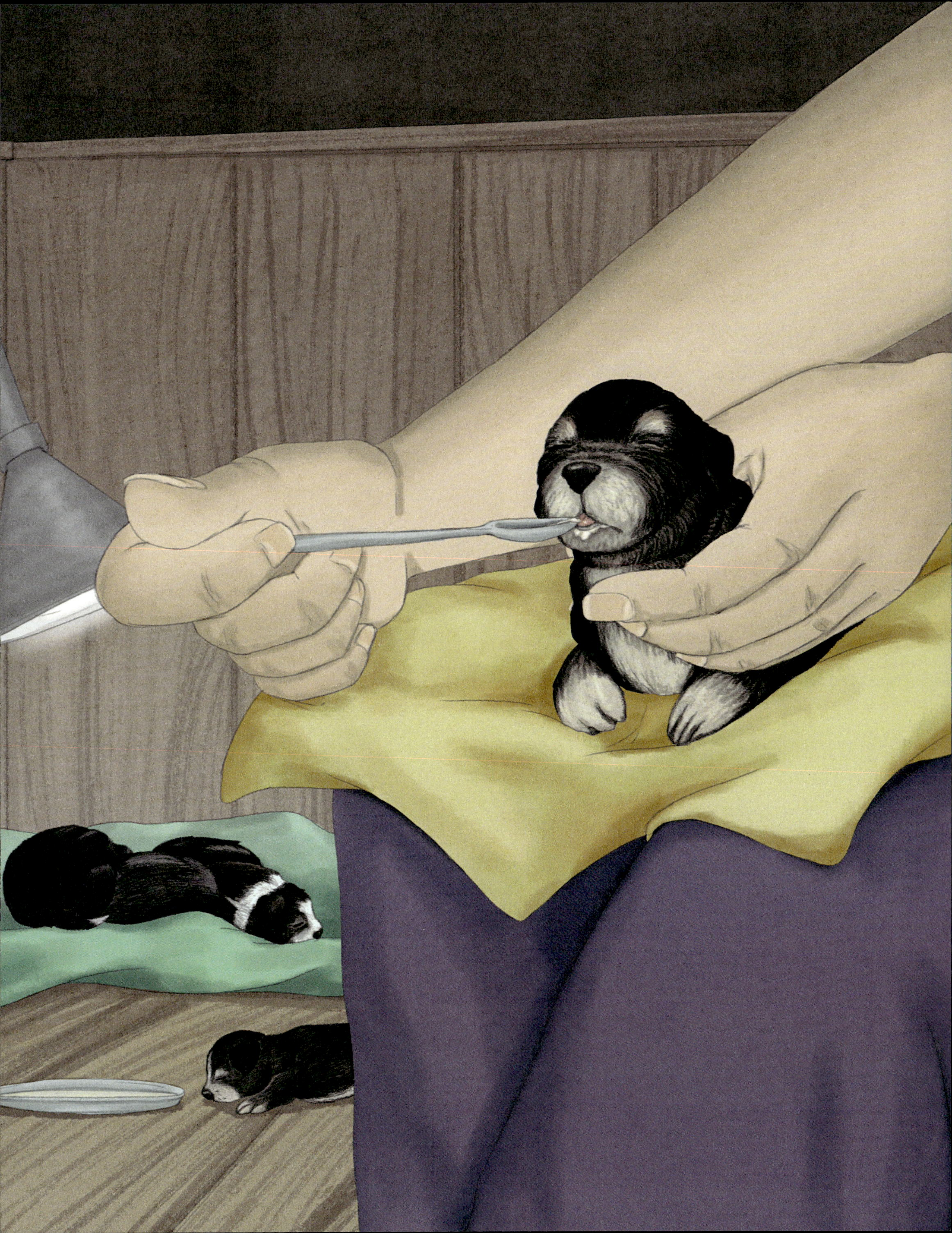

My siblings and I woke the next morning to the sound of the Farm Lady's voice. We all had much more energy thanks to our dinner and a good night's sleep. As the Farm Lady approached, we could all smell our next meal. She set down a bowl of warm milk and left the stall. This time, we did a bit better at lapping up the milk in the bowl. It just took a little practice. I looked at my sister Abby. "Are we out of danger yet? Are we going to be OK?" I questioned.

"I think so," affirmed Abby, but I couldn't tell if she was sure.

Then I saw the stall door slowly open, and a huge black Labrador with a red bandanna around her neck quietly crept in!

"We are in danger!" I whispered to Abby in fear.

"We are not in danger, Ranger. Now, shhhhhh. She might be nice."

We all were very still as the large Lab headed straight toward us. I began to shake in fear. The giant Lab stopped at our food bowl and began to noisily lap up the milk.

"Maggie!" I heard the Farm Lady say from inside the barn. "You better not be in that stall eating their food!" she warned. The Lab took a few more licks from the bowl and then began to back up toward the door. Just before she backed out of sight, she looked straight at me, and her tail gave a friendly wag. I wagged back.

Maggie visited us every time the Farm Lady lost track of her, licking our bowls clean when we were finished. I looked forward to her visits because she would often lick our faces and clean each pup up, just like Mama did. We became especially good friends the day I got brave and chased after her tail. I thought I might be in trouble with her because she quickly turned around toward me, but she gently picked me up by the scruff of my neck, set me back down, and playfully rolled me around with her nose. Maggie and I became the best of friends.

Maggie always came down to the barn with Bella, a five-year-old purebred border collie and the self-appointed manager of the farm. Bella also wore a red bandanna and loved to work. She didn't spend much time playing with us, but she was kind and very smart. Bella told me all about Chase, the border collie who used to run the whole farm but was much older now and preferred to stay up near the house. He was still admired by Bella and Maggie. Maggie told me that Bella really missed running and playing with him on the farm.

As each of us pups began to get bigger and stronger, it was clear that Abby and I were going to be much larger than the others. Abby looked just like a purebred border collie, but I was brown, with freckles on my long and lanky legs, a white chest, a brown tail with a white tip, and the goofiest ears you have ever seen. The Farm Lady would laugh at my goofy ears and say, "Ranger, those silly ears of yours!" My ears lay awkwardly on top of my head, with one ear going forward and the other going back.

The Farm Lady promised to find each of us a forever home that would be just right for us. As we began to eat dog food on our own and grew to be several months old, one by one my siblings found homes, and our large litter began to shrink until there was just Abby and me.One afternoon when I was lying in the sun with Maggie, Bella, and Abby, a car drove up and met the Farm Lady at the barn gate.

"It must be someone to adopt one of us," said Abby. "I really want to go to my forever home; don't you, Ranger?"

I could not answer; I just scooted over toward Maggie and laid my head on her back, hoping the Farm Lady didn't see me.

Bella, being wise and kind, was the first to notice that I was afraid and didn't want to be chosen.

"You are not in danger, Ranger. The Farm Lady promised to find the perfect home for you," Bella said warmly.

"I don't want to leave you and Maggie. I don't want to leave the farm. I love rolling in the grass, digging holes, and chasing the goats. I'm scared I won't like my forever home," I explained through tears.

"Ranger," said Bella softly, "I know you had some scary things happen in your short puppy life, and it is always good to be cautious, but just because something is new and even a little scary does not mean you are in danger."

Bella then scooted next to me and lay down. I felt safe with her. I knew Bella was right, and I remembered the Farm Lady's promise to find the perfect home for me.

As the four of us pups huddled together, the Farm Lady and the visitor approached us with kindness in their eyes.

"I have found the perfect forever home for Abby and for you as well, Ranger," announced the Farm Lady.

My mind raced, and although I felt relieved that at least I would get to live with Abby, I felt a lump in my throat, and I hung my head in despair at the thought of living away from my best friend, Maggie. As I quickly looked at Maggie, I could see the sadness in her brave eyes, too, as she sat up close to me. We both knew this day would come.

Abby jumped up and enthusiastically followed the visitor toward her car, and I reluctantly followed along, with Maggie by my side. Abby jumped in excitedly, but before I could get in, the Farm Lady told me to say goodbye to Abby as she shut the car door. As the car drove off, Abby and I both barked goodbye. The Farm Lady turned to me and looked right into my eyes. She then leaned over and tied a matching red bandanna around my neck and said the finest words I have ever heard in my short puppy life: "Ranger, the perfect forever home for you is here on the ranch with Maggie and Bella. Now go play, you sweet little pup." Then she gave me a pat on my head and a sweet kiss.

RES-QME

I looked over at Maggie, and her eyes were as big and wide as mine! "Woo-hoo!" my heart said as Maggie and I took off toward the barn to share the great news with Bella. When Bella saw my bandanna, she knew. She took a break from her chores and chased the fence lines with us, and we played together happily. Maggie tossed me around on the soft farm grass with her nose. I tugged on her neck as we ran and played until we had no energy left.

That night, I got to sleep up at the house with Bella and Maggie. We cuddled together, and I laid my head on Maggie's back. The Farm Lady had kept her promise. This was the perfect home for me. No more danger for Ranger.

The Real Ranger as a Pup

the Lady
Barrow

The Real Maggie

The Real Bella

Made in the USA
San Bernardino, CA
24 January 2017